TH

S.

AND THE SECOND VATICAN COUNCIL

SOME OTHER TITLES
By the Same Author

THE CATHOLIC SANCTUARY

AND THE SECOND VATICAN COUNCIL

By

Michael Davies

"I have loved, O Lord, the beauty of thy house; and the place where thy glory dwelleth." —Psalm 25:8

TAN Books
Charlotte, North Carolina

Library of Congress Catalog Card No.: 96-61969

ISBN 0-89555-547-6

Cover photo: Sanctuary of The Oratory, Brompton Road, London, with permission of the Superior.

Printed and bound in the United States of America.

Published in the United States by
TAN Books
PO Box 410487
Charlotte, NC 28241
www.TANBooks.com

"A real change in the contemporary perception of the purpose of the Mass and the Eucharist will occur only when the table altars are removed and Mass is again celebrated at the high altar; when the purpose of the Mass is again seen as an act of adoration and glorification of God and of offering thanks for His blessings, for our salvation and for the promise of the heavenly life to come, and as the mystical reenactment of the Lord's sacrifice on the cross."

—Msgr. Klaus Gamber
*The Reform of the
Roman Liturgy* (1993), p.175

THE CATHOLIC
SANCTUARY

AND THE SECOND VATICAN COUNCIL

In the Traditional Mass of the Roman Rite the Catholic priest offers Mass in a sacred place, a sanctuary, set apart from the rest of the church for sacrifice, as was the Holy of Holies in the Jewish Temple, to which the celebrant refers explicitly in the silent prayer *Aufer a nobis* as he ascends to the altar of sacrifice: "Take away from us our iniquities, we beseech Thee, O Lord, that with pure minds we may enter the Holy of Holies." As he recites this prayer the celebrant is filled with the thought of the holiness of God and the awesome nature of the mysteries that he is about to celebrate.

Throughout the centuries the Catholic people have spared no effort and no expense to build sanctuaries which provided a worthy setting for the awesome Sacrifice, sanctuaries which provided a foretaste of the true Holy of Holies, Heaven itself. In the Eastern Churches the faithful are not even permitted to witness the most solemn moment of the liturgy as it takes place behind the ikonostasis. However, in the past three decades tens of thousands of exquisite Catholic sanctuaries have been destroyed—in obedience, it is claimed, to the requirements of the Second Vatican Council. Before examining this claim it is necessary to make a brief examination of liturgical development in the Church.

The early Christians assembled for divine worship in the house of one of their number who possessed a large dining room. The reason was, of course, that as a persecuted minority the Christians could erect no public buildings. A number of present-day churches in Rome bear the name of Christians in that locality who had dwellings where Mass was celebrated in the first centuries. Mass was also celebrated in the Roman catacombs on the tombs of the martyrs, which gave rise to the practice of imbedding the relics of martyrs in the altár when Christians were eventually allowed to build churches.

Our knowledge of the way Mass was celebrated increases with each succeeding century, since there is a gradual and natural development, with the prayers and formulas and eventually the ceremonial actions developing into set forms. The only liturgical book used up to the fourth century was the Bible, and we have no actual copies of liturgical books extant prior to the seventh century.

Historical factors played a crucial role in the manner in which the liturgy was celebrated. During times of persecution, brevity and simplicity were its principal characteristics, for obvious reasons. The toleration of Christianity under Constantine I (324-337) and its adoption as the religion of the Empire under Theodosius I (379-395) had a dramatic effect on the development of Christian ritual. Congregations increased in size, and benefactions for the building and furnishing of churches resulted in the enrichment of vessels and vestments. Those presenting such gifts would naturally want them to be the richest and most beautiful possible. In a parallel development, the liturgical rites became more elaborate, with solemn processions and stress upon the awesome nature of the rite. This elaboration of the liturgy during the fourth century came about throughout the Christian world as the result of the liturgy's change from an illegal and private ritual into a state-supported and public one.

THE MASS FACING EAST

The most important consideration in the building of churches and the construction of sanctuaries was the fact that, in the East and in the West, Mass was always celebrated facing eastward. The rising of the sun in the East each day was seen as a symbol of the Resurrection of the Saviour and of His Second Coming. St. John Damascene (c. 675-c. 749) wrote:

> At His ascent into Heaven He went to the East, and so do the Apostles pray to Him; He will come again as the Apostles saw Him going, and so the Lord Himself says: "As the lightning comes forth from the East and shines even to the West, so shall the coming of the Son of Man be." Since we wait for Him, we pray toward the East. This is the unwritten tradition of the Apostles.

The Second Coming was awaited with great eagerness by the early Christians; whereas today, alas, it is something to which the typical Catholic rarely if ever devotes a moment's thought. The East was also seen as a symbol of Heaven, the Jerusalem above, in contrast to the Jerusalem below, toward which the Jews turned in worship.

An erroneous argument put forward by proponents of Mass facing the people is that "Christ, whom the priest represents at Mass, did not sit with His back to the Apostles at the Last Supper." Quite true, but neither did He face them across a table. They all reclined on the same side of the table, facing Jerusalem, just as for nearly 2,000 years of Christian history priest and people have offered or assisted at Mass on the same side of the altar, facing the East. Nor, incidentally, was the Last Supper a vernacular celebration. The liturgical language of Hebrew was used, which was as different from the everyday Aramaic used by the Jews at that time as Latin is from contemporary French.

Archaeological research proves that from the moment the Christians were allowed to build churches, they always did so along an east-west axis. By the end of the fourth century, it was an invariable rule in the East that churches should be built with the apse (the semicircular end which houses the altar) at the east end, and the same procedure had been adopted in the West by the second half of the fifth century.

A small number of the more ancient churches in the West, in Rome in particular, still had an apse at the west end. But where this was the case, the altar would be constructed so that the celebrant could stand on the west side of it and thus offer the Sacrifice facing the East. He would indeed be facing the people; however, his purpose would not be to celebrate Mass toward them but rather to celebrate the Eucharistic liturgy facing the East. During the first part of the Mass, the Liturgy of the Catechumens, the people would face the altar to hear the readings and the homily. At the end of the Mass of the Catechumens, the celebrant would say, *"Conversi ad Dominum"*—"Turn

toward the Lord"—which meant "Turn to face
the East." Then, for the duration of the
Eucharistic liturgy, the people would turn to
face the East, men on one side of the church
and women on the other, and hence they would
have their backs to the altar.

PROTESTANT HATRED OF THE MASS

Before examining what Vatican II mandated
concerning the sanctuary, reference must be
made to a widespread abandonment of the eastward celebration of the Eucharist which took
place 400 years before this Council was con-
voked. This was a step taken by the Protestant
Reformers in the sixteenth century. The use of
the word "Reformers" for these people is certainly a misnomer. In reality, they were not
reformers, but revolutionaries of the first
order—men out to overthrow the existing religion and replace it with one which they had
fabricated themselves on the grounds that it
conformed to the teaching and practice of primitive Christianity.

The Protestant Reformers were united in
abolishing the eastward celebration of the
Eucharist because they understood, quite correctly, that the eastward direction signified sacrifice, and the denial of the sacrificial nature of
the Mass was an axiom upon which the entire

Protestant heresy was based. Martin Luther regarded the concept of any true sacrifice in the Mass as an abomination, and he expressed his viewpoint in the forceful manner for which he was noted:

It is indeed upon the Mass as on a rock that the whole papal system is built, with its monasteries, its bishoprics, its collegiate churches, its altars, its ministries, its doctrine, i.e., with all its guts. All these cannot fail to crumble once their sacrilegious and abominable Mass falls.[1]

This viewpoint is put even more forcefully by John Hooper, the Anglican Bishop of Gloucester in the reign of Edward VI (1547-1553):

I believe and confess that the popish Mass is an invention and ordinance of man, a sacrifice of Antichrist, and a forsaking of the sacrifice of Jesus Christ, that is to say, of his death and passion; and that it is a stinking and infected sepulchre, which hideth and covereth the merit of the blood of Christ; and therefore ought the Mass to be abolished and the holy supper of the Lord to be restored and set in its perfection again.[2]

Because Protestants believed the Mass to be a sacrifice of Antichrist, they did indeed abolish it, replacing it with a communion service, a mere meal, a Lord's Supper in which Our Lord is present only in the minds of the congregation. The Real Presence was replaced by a Real Absence.

In order to eradicate any memory of the hated Mass from the minds of the faithful, the Reformers resolved to obliterate every vestige of it from their communion services and from the sanctuaries in which the Sacrifice had been offered for centuries. The program of Thomas Cranmer, the apostate Archbishop of Canterbury, in the reign of the puppet boy-king Edward VI (1547-1553), has been summarized perfectly by Dr. Eamon Duffy in his recent and remarkable book, *The Stripping of the Altars.* This book has been universally acclaimed as a classic of historical research, and all who read it have been struck by the fact that it could be describing what has happened throughout the Catholic world since the Second Vatican Council. Dr. Duffy writes:

At the heart of the Edwardine reform was the necessity of destroying, of cutting, hammering, scraping, or melting into a deserved oblivion the monuments of popery, so that the doctrines they embodied might be forgotten. Iconoclasm was the central sacrament of the reform, and, as the programme of the leaders became more radical in the years between 1547 and 1553, they sought with greater urgency the celebration of that sacrament of forgetfulness in every parish in the land. The churchwardens' accounts of the period witness a wholesale removal of the images, vestments, and vessels which had been the wonder of foreign visitors to the country, and in which the collective memory of the parishes were, quite literally, enshrined.[3]

THE SMASHING OF ALTARS

The replacement of altars by tables was the first objective of the English Protestants, and this was fully in line with what had taken place in continental Europe. Calvin taught that since Christ has accomplished His sacrifice once and for all, God "hath given us a table at which we are to feast, not an altar upon which any victim is to be offered: he hath not consecrated priests to offer sacrifices, but ministers to distribute the sacred banquet."[4] This was of course a direct contradiction of the traditional Christian teaching, handed down from the Apostles, that the Eucharist is a sacrifice—the renewal of the one Sacrifice of Calvary—as well as a sacred banquet. In the New Testament St. Paul uses the term "altar" (*Heb.* 13:10) as well as the term "table of the Lord" (*1 Cor.* 1:21) when referring to the Holy Eucharist.

On November 24, 1550, the King's Council ordered the destruction of all the altars throughout the kingdom. In the future the "Lord's Supper" was to be celebrated on a table covered with a cloth of linen.[5] The most notorious altar-smasher in England and Wales was Nicholas Ridley, the Anglican Bishop of London. A letter sent to Ridley by the Council in the name of the King included certain "Reasons why the Lord's Board should rather be after the form of a Table than an Altar." Among the reasons given were the following:

First, the form of a table shall more move the simple from the superstitious opinions of the Popish mass unto the right use of the Lord's Supper. For the use of an altar is to make sacrifice upon it: the use of a table is to serve for men to eat upon.[6]

A descendant of Bishop Ridley states, in a biography of his reforming ancestor, that the destruction of the altars was considered as sacrilege by the ordinary people and shocked them into a realization of the full extent of the revolution which had taken place. J. G. Ridley writes:

The removal of altars brought home to every subject in the kingdom that the central object which had stood in the churches for over a thousand years, and which they had watched with awe every Sunday since their early childhood, was condemned as idolatrous and thrown contemptuously away by adherents of the new religion which had been forced upon them.[7]

How sad it is that countless Catholic bishops in our time have emulated Nicholas Ridley and thrown away contemptuously the altar which the faithful of their dioceses have watched with awe every Sunday since their early childhood. Commenting on the destruction of the consecrated altars of the Christian sacrifice throughout England and Wales, Fr. T. E. Bridgett writes:

Wherever churchwardens' accounts exist, we find entries similar to this of Burnham in Buckinghamshire: "Payd to tylars for breckynge downe forten (14) awters in the cherche." It is only from such scraps of history that we can rebuild and repeople in imagination the interior of the desolate old churches where countless Masses were once offered.[8]

Is it not heartbreaking that since the Second

Vatican Council, in countless churches and cathedrals, there are entries in the accounts stating that vast sums of money have been spent in destroying beautiful altars on which countless Masses have been offered?

DESTRUCTION OF ALTARS, DESTRUCTION OF THE LITURGY

The rite of Mass which had once been celebrated in the devastated sanctuaries was destroyed by the Protestant Reformers as ruthlessly and totally as the altars upon which it was celebrated. The sublime Latin prayers of the traditional Mass, which dated back to the sixth century and beyond, into the mists of antiquity, were replaced by an English service from which every specifically sacrificial prayer had been removed. Because the Mass is a solemn sacrifice offered to God by the priest in the person of Christ, many of the prayers— addressed directly to God—had been spoken inaudibly. The Protestant Lord's Supper was not a mystical sacrifice, a mystery, but a meal and a service of prayers and instruction, so it was mandated that every word spoken was to be heard by all the people. Communion on the tongue was replaced by Communion in the hand to make it clear that the bread received was ordinary bread and that the minister who distributed it was an ordinary man, not a priest. Communion under one kind was replaced by Communion under both kinds, because in every meal there should be both food and drink. Above all, the never-to-be-sufficiently-exe-crated eastward position of the celebrant at Mass was to be abandoned forever.

One of the most appalling consequences of the change from a Latin to a vernacular liturgy was that it cut the Catholic people off completely from the entire liturgical and musical heritage of Western Christendom. Dr. Eamon Duffy comments:

> The switch from Latin to English immediately rendered obsolete the entire musical repertoire of cathedral, chapel, and parish church. Not least of the shocks brought on by the Prayer Book at Whitsun 1549 must have been the silencing of all but a handful of choirs and the reduction of the liturgy on one of the greatest festivals of the year to a monotone dialogue between curate and clerk.[9]

Has not this also happened today? At a time when young people in the West are flocking to record shops to buy compact discs by the million of our Gregorian musical heritage, that heritage has been banished from almost all the Catholic churches in the English-speaking world—despite the fact that Vatican II mandated it as the norm for sung Masses. ("Constitution on the Sacred Liturgy," Art. 116). One wonders why so many bishops claiming to be loyal to the Council do not obey it in this important matter.

The Reformation in England by Msgr. Philip Hughes is the most authoritative account of the English Reformation yet written. Msgr. Hughes proves beyond any doubt that the faith of the Catholic people was destroyed primarily by liturgical changes, and he insists Cranmer's *Book of Common Prayer* was a prime instrument in this destruction:

> Once these new sacramental rites had become the habit of the English people, the substance of the doctrinal reformation, victorious now in northern Europe, would have transformed England also. All but insensibly, as the years went by, the beliefs enshrined in the old, and now disused, rites, and kept alive by these rites in men's minds and affections, would disappear—without the need of any systematic missionary effort to preach them down.[10]

Monsignor Hughes is referring here to a principle fundamental to every form of liturgy: *Lex orandi, lex credendi*—"The law of prayer is the law of belief." This means that the manner in which people pray will determine what they believe. As Msgr. Hughes has explained, when the traditional Latin liturgical rites were replaced by new vernacular services, when the altars were replaced by tables, and when the celebrant turned to face the people, then almost imperceptibly, as the years passed by, the people, who were praying as Protestants, began to believe as Protestants.

CLEAR DISTINCTION BETWEEN CATHOLIC WORSHIP AND PROTESTANT WORSHIP

The line of demarcation between Catholic and Protestant worship was laid down clearly at the Reformation. The most striking differences were as follows: The Catholic Mass was celebrated in Latin; the Protestant Lord's Supper in English. Much of the Mass was celebrated in an inaudible tone; the Lord's Supper was spoken audibly throughout. The Mass began with the Psalm *Judica me,* in which the priest stated specifically that he was going unto the altar of God, and ended with the sublime Last Gospel; in the Lord's Supper the *Judica me* and the Last Gospel and many traditional prayers were abolished, particularly the sacrificial Offertory Prayers. The Mass was celebrated on a sacrificial altar facing the East; the

Lord's Supper was celebrated on a table facing the people. In the Mass, Holy Communion was placed on the tongue of the communicant by the anointed hand of a priest; in the Lord's Supper it was placed in the hand of the communicant. In the Mass, Holy Communion was given to the laity under one kind only; in the Lord's Supper it was always administered under both kinds.

This clear distinction between Catholic and Protestant worship remained unchanged for four centuries (until the Second Vatican Council), making it clear, as John Henry Cardinal Newman expressed it, that Catholicism and Protestantism are two different religions, and not two ways of expressing the same faith.

NOT MANDATED BY VATICAN II

This brings us at last to the Second Vatican Council, which was held in Rome in four sessions between the years 1962 and 1965. The teaching of the Council on liturgical reform is contained in its "Constitution on the Sacred Liturgy"—*Sacrosanctum Concilium*—which is dated December 4, 1963. What precisely does the Liturgy Constitution mandate regarding changes in our sanctuaries? The answer is brief and simple: Nothing!

There is not a single word in the entire Liturgy Constitution of Vatican Council II requiring a single change to be made in a single sanctuary anywhere in the entire Catholic world.

As very few Catholics have read the Liturgy Constitution, it will be useful to examine precisely what it actually mandated. By no possible stretch of the imagination can it be interpreted as mandating, sanctioning or even envisaging the virtual destruction of the traditional Roman Rite of the Mass or of the sanctuaries in which it was celebrated.

The Liturgy Constitution contained stipulations which appeared to rule out the least possibility of any drastic remodeling of the traditional Mass or the sanctuaries in which it was celebrated. The Latin language was to be preserved in the Latin rites (Article 36), and steps were to be taken to ensure that the faithful could sing or say together in Latin those parts of the Mass that pertain to them (Article 54). All lawfully acknowledged rites were held to be of equal authority and dignity and were to be preserved in the future and fostered in every way (Article 4). The treasury of sacred music was to be preserved and fostered with great care (Article 114), and Gregorian chant was to be given pride of place in liturgical services (Article 116). There were to be no innovations unless the good of the Church genuinely and certainly required them (Article 23).

The Council Fathers thus had no fears that the immemorial rite of Mass, "The most beautiful thing this side of Heaven," according to Fr. Frederick Faber, would be subjected to revolutionary changes that would leave it virtually unrecognizable. They would never have voted for the reform that has been inflicted upon us. You do not need to take my word for this. I will quote one of the greatest liturgists of this century, perhaps the greatest, the late Msgr. Klaus Gamber. His book, *The Reform of the Roman Liturgy,* was published in English in 1993 and is endorsed by three cardinals. Shortly before the death of Msgr. Gamber, Cardinal Ratzinger, the present Prefect of the Sacred Congregation for the Doctrine of the Faith, remarked that he was "the one scholar who, among the army of pseudo-liturgists, truly represents the liturgical thinking of the centre of the Church." [11] It is the army of pseudo-liturgists referred to by the Cardinal which has invaded and devastated our sanctuaries. "One statement we can make with certainty," writes Msgr. Gamber, "is that the new *Ordo* of the Mass that has now emerged would not have been endorsed by the majority of the Council Fathers." [12]

Precisely the same point was made by Cardinal John Heenan of Westminster, who explains in his book, *A Crown of Thorns,* that

The subject most fully debated was

liturgical reform. It might be more accurate to say that the bishops were under the impression that the liturgy had been fully discussed. In retrospect it is clear that they were given the opportunity of discussing only general principles. *Subsequent changes were more radical than those intended by Pope John and the bishops who passed the decree on the liturgy. His sermon at the end of the first session shows that Pope John did not suspect what was being planned by the liturgical experts* [my emphasis].[13]

THE "LITURGICAL EXPERTS" TAKE OVER

Cardinal Heenan's reference to "liturgical experts" is crucial if we are to understand the reason for the orgy of destruction in our sanctuaries which followed the Council. Those who exercised the greatest influence during Vatican II were not the Council Fathers, the three thousand bishops and heads of religious orders who had come to Rome from all over the world, but the expert advisers they brought with them, referred to in Latin as the *periti*. Bishop Lucey of Cork and Ross stated explicitly that the *periti* were the people with power.[14] Cardinal Heenan warned that when the Council was over the *periti* were planning to use the Council documents in a manner which the Council Fathers had not envisaged. The documents were to be interpreted and implemented by commissions to be established after the Council. Cardinal Heenan warned against the danger of the *periti* taking control of these commissions, thus gaining the power to interpret the Council to the world. "God forbid that this should happen!" he cried—but happen it did.[15]

Article 128 of the Liturgy Constitution provides a typical example. It reads:

The canons and ecclesiastical statutes which govern the provision of external things which pertain to sacred worship should be revised as soon as possible, together with the liturgical books, as laid down in Article 25. These laws refer especially to the worthy and well-planned construction of sacred buildings, the shape and construction of altars, the nobility, placing, and security of the eucharistic tabernacle, the suitability and dignity of the baptistry, the proper ordering of sacred images, and the scheme of decoration and embellishment. Laws which seem less suited to the reformed liturgy should be amended or abolished. Those which are helpful are to be retained, or introduced if lacking.

Looked at with the benefit of hindsight this passage provides an open-ended mandate for drastic change. Read the passage carefully; all its objectives are admirable, and what possible reason could bishops who "did not suspect what was being planned by the liturgical experts" have had for objecting to it? Every Catholic must wish to see worthy and well planned sacred buildings. The bishops could not possibly have foreseen an epidemic of churches which resemble badly designed airport carparks. This is particularly the case in view of the safeguards which are listed above on page 17.

The commission established to implement the Liturgy Constitution was known as the *Consilium,* and it took the extraordinary step of asking six Protestants—six heretics—to advise them in drawing up their plans to reform the liturgy of the Mass, which has been the principal object of Protestant hatred since the time of Martin Luther. These Protestants played a very active part in all the discussions on the reform of the liturgy, as one of them confirmed in a letter to me.[16]

The fact that the Liturgy Constitution did not mandate any changes in the sanctuary did not in the least daunt the pseudo-liturgists once the Council was over and the bishops had returned to their dioceses. A seemingly endless series of documents was generated, and is still being generated, by the vast liturgical bureaucracy that has proliferated since the Council.

THE COUNCIL MISQUOTED BY THE SACRED CONGREGATION OF RITES

Where changes in the sanctuary are concerned, the first mention is found in the "Instruction on the Proper Implementation of the Constitution on the Sacred Liturgy" (*Inter Oecumenici*) published by the Sacred Congregation of Rites on September 26, 1964. This document is now generally referred to as the "First Instruction," as others were to follow. Paragraph 90 of this document reads:

> In building new churches and in repairing or adapting old ones, care must be taken to ensure that they lend themselves to the celebration of the divine services as these are meant to be celebrated, and to achieve the active participation of the faithful.

The Instruction claims that this is a quotation from Article 124 of the Liturgy Constitution— but it is not. The Liturgy Constitution refers only to the building of *new* churches and makes no reference whatsoever to repairing or adapting existing buildings.

It is this one word, "adapting," inserted into

the First Instruction, thus misquoting the Liturgy Constitution, which forms the basis of the altar-smashers' mandate.

Having stated incorrectly that the Council authorized the adaptation of existing churches, the Instruction goes on in the very next paragraph, No. 91, to state:

> It is better for the high altar to be constructed away from the wall so that one can move round it without difficulty, and so that it can be used for a celebration facing the people.

This is the first reference to Mass facing the people, and note well that it is only a suggestion that altars should be constructed away from the wall to make such a celebration possible. It does not actually recommend that Mass should ever be offered facing the people. In countries such as Holland, however, a veritable orgy of altar smashing was already underway, causing such scandal that in 1965 Cardinal Lercaro, President of the Consilium, found it necessary to write to the presidents of episcopal conferences stressing the fact that there was no pastoral necessity for Mass to be celebrated facing the people and expressing regret at the hasty and irreparable destruction of existing altars, violating values which should be respected.[17]

On May 25, 1967, in the Instruction *Eucha-*

risticum Mysterium published by the Sacred Congregation of Rites, it was stated specifically that "In adapting churches, care will be taken not to destroy treasures of sacred art" (par. 24). I well recollect reading in the newsletter of a parish in southeast London an account of a Protestant stonemason who had been heartbroken at having to smash an exquisitely beautiful marble altar in a convent and to replace it with what he described as "two great hunks of stone." As a true craftsman, he found the task utterly repugnant, particularly as he was sure that there is not a stonemason in Britain who could produce such superb work today. The worthy gentleman would have been even more surprised had he been told that this act of vandalism was intended to promote the renewal of Catholic worship. What sort of renewal can be implemented only by destroying the holy and the beautiful? To quote Dr. Duffy once more: "Iconoclasm was the central sacrament of the reform."

ANOTHER MISQUOTATION

The next significant document is the "General Instruction on the Roman Missal," published in April of 1969. Article 262 of this Instruction, while purporting to quote Article 91 of the First Instruction, actually misquotes it. Article 262 reads:

The high altar should be constructed away from the wall so that one can move round it without difficulty, and so that it can be used for a celebration facing the people.

We thus have the suggestion found in the First Instruction, "It is better for the high altar to be constructed away from the wall" ("*Praestat ut altare maius exstruatur a pariete seiunctum . . .*") misquoted by omitting "*Praestat ut*" ("It is better that") so that it becomes an implied command: "*Altare maius exstruatur a pariete seiunctum . . .*" ("The high altar should be constructed away from the wall . . ."). The Liturgy Constitution was thus misquoted in the First Instruction, and the First Instruction is misquoted in the General Instruction. However, despite this misquotation, by no possible stretch of the imagination can Article 262 of the General Instruction be interpreted as mandating the destruction of existing altars to make possible a celebration facing the people. Interpreted in the light of the authentic text of Article 124 of the Liturgy Constitution, it can only refer to the construction of altars in new churches, not the demolition of altars in existing churches.

POPE PAUL VI'S RUBRICS PRESUME MASS FACING THE ALTAR

There is, in fact, irrefutable proof that, whatever the intentions of the pseudo-liturgists, the mind of the Pope was that the New Mass should *not* be celebrated facing the people.

The rubrics of the New Mass, approved specifically by Pope Paul VI, presume that the priest will be facing the altar in the traditional manner as the norm for its celebration. The rubrics of the 1970 Missal instruct the priest to turn to the congregation at specific moments of the Mass and then to turn back to face the altar, e.g., Nos. 2, 25, 104, 105, 111 and 113. These rubrics can also be found in the General Instruction, Nos. 107, 115, 116, 122, 198 and 199. Where the rubrics governing the actual celebration of Mass are concerned, both in the Order of Mass and in the General Instruction, *there is not one which envisages a celebration facing the people!*

Msgr. Klaus Gamber, quoted earlier, stated, "One would look in vain for a statement in the Constitution on the Sacred Liturgy of the Second Vatican Council that said that Holy Mass is to be celebrated facing the people."[18]

NO MANDATORY CHANGES

Anyone wishing to see a famous church which has stuck to the letter of the law in reordering its sanctuary and made only those changes which are mandatory should visit the Brompton Oratory in London. The Oratorian Fathers are certainly the most liturgically literate group of priests in Britain, and they have not made a single change in their sanctuary because there is no law requiring them to do so. Their magnificent altar stands just as it always has, with the prominent tabernacle in the center.

Cardinal Ratzinger—who as head of the Sacred Congregation for the Doctrine of the Faith is second only to the Pope in his authority in the Church—stated recently that the change to Mass facing the people was a mistake. Asked to comment, Paolo Portoghesi, one of the greatest architects in the world, with a specialized knowledge of ecclesiastical architecture, said he was in full agreement with the Cardinal and admired his courageous stand.[19] It may well be that we are on the verge of a return to liturgical sanity, what Cardinal Ratzinger has termed "a reform of the reform."

On Friday, October 21, 1995, I visited the chapel of the American College in Rome where, at the request of the seminarians, the tabernacle has recently been restored to its traditional place of honor in the center of the high altar. This would certainly not have been done if mandatory legislation existed requiring it to be situated elsewhere.

On Saturday, October 22, 1995, during a meeting with Cardinal Ratzinger, I informed him of what had happened in the American College, and he expressed great pleasure at the news. I asked the Cardinal whether any sanctuary changes had actually been mandated by the Liturgy Constitution or post-conciliar legislation. He assured me that in this legislation there exists no mandate, in the primary sense of the term as a command, to rearrange sanctuaries. While such changes may have been inspired by the liturgical reform they could not be said to be required by the legislation of the Church. The Cardinal gave me his permission to quote him to this effect.

THE PRESIDENT'S CHAIR

Another argument in favor of altar-smashing can be disposed of easily. Article 271 of the General Instruction states that the celebrant's chair should draw attention to his office of presiding over the community and leading its prayer, and hence the place for it is the apex of the sanctuary, facing the people. One must state immediately that this is a description of the function of a Protestant minister and not of a Catholic priest, whose office is not to preside over the community but to offer the Holy Sacrifice *in persona Christi* ("in the person of Christ"). But leaving that aside, Article 271 states specifically that there are circumstances which might militate against the presidential chair being at the apex of the sanctuary, and therefore this cannot be considered mandatory.

There is thus no mandatory legislation within the Church today requiring that Mass be celebrated facing the people, let alone that sanctuaries be vandalized. Bishops who emulate 16th-century Protestant Bishop Ridley in smashing hallowed altars built with the pennies of the poor do so not because they have to, but because they want to!

THE ERROR OF "ARCHAEOLOGISM"

Modern liturgists may claim that these changes bring us closer to the way the first Christians worshipped. This may be true, but as I have pointed out, the early Christians worshipped in the way they did—using a table, for example—because they were a persecuted minority, forbidden to build places of worship. Once the persecution ended, they built churches which were a fitting setting for the Holy Sacri-

fice of the Mass, which was offered in an
increasingly elaborate rite inspired by the desire
to render the greatest possible glory to God, to
whom all honor is due. The way one worships
in a time of persecution cannot be considered
the norm for a time of freedom.

The theory that the older a liturgical practice
is the better it is was condemned unequivocally
by Pope Pius XII, the greatest and most erudite
Pontiff of this century, who possessed an unri-
valed knowledge of the principles of sound
liturgy. In his encyclical *Mediator Dei,* published in 1947, he wrote:

> The liturgy of the early ages is worthy
> of veneration; but an ancient custom is not
> to be considered better, either in itself or
> in relation to later times and circum-
> stances, just because it has the flavor of
> antiquity . . . The desire to restore every-
> thing indiscriminately to its ancient con-
> dition is neither wise nor praiseworthy . . .
> It would be wrong, for example, to want
> the altar restored to its ancient form of
> table; to want black eliminated from the
> liturgical colors, and pictures and statues
> excluded from our churches; to require
> crucifixes that do not represent the bitter
> sufferings of the divine Redeemer . . .
> This attitude is an attempt to revive the
> "archaeologism" to which the pseudo-

synod of Pistoia (1794) gave rise; it seeks also to re-introduce the many pernicious errors which led to that synod and resulted from it and which the Church, in her capacity of watchful guardian of "the Deposit of Faith" entrusted to her by her divine Founder, has rightly condemned. It is a wicked movement, that tends to paralyze the sanctifying and salutary action by which the liturgy leads the children of adoption on the path to their heavenly Father (pars. 65-68).

PLACEMENT OF THE TABERNACLE

This condemnation of Pope Pius XII was aimed at an influential faction within the hitherto papally approved liturgical movement. Pope Pius did not hesitate to denounce in the strongest possible terms certain theories and practices promoted by this faction: "false, dangerous, pernicious, a wicked movement, a false doctrine that distorts the Catholic notion of faith itself." One of the pernicious theses it promoted was that the impact of the Sacrifice of the Mass was lessened if Our Lord were already present in a tabernacle upon the altar. But in an address to a liturgical congress in Assisi in 1956, this great Pope warned that their true motivation was to lessen esteem "for the presence and action of Christ in the tabernacle." He insisted, correctly, that "To separate tabernacle from altar is to separate two things which by their origin and nature should remain united." If this was true in 1956, it is still true today. It is to be regretted that one of the post-conciliar documents has actually suggested that "it is more in keeping with the nature of the celebration" not to have the Blessed Sacrament reserved on the altar from the beginning of Mass.[20]

There is not one word requiring the demoting of the tabernacle in any document of the Second Vatican Council. The tabernacle is referred to in a passage of Article 128 which says that ecclesiastical laws governing liturgical externals should be revised as soon as possible, in accord with the revised liturgy. Such laws were to be amended, abolished, retained, or introduced if lacking. These laws included those relating to "the nobility, placing, and security of the eucharistic tabernacle."

As noted earlier, this passage provides a typical example of what Cardinal Heenan warned against (see pp. 18-19 above), that is, the manner in which the liturgical experts inserted phrases into the Liturgy Constitution which they could interpret after the Council in a manner that neither Pope John nor the Council Fathers suspected could possibly happen. Every Catholic must be concerned with "the nobility, placing, and security" of the tabernacle. The bishops could not possibly have suspected the demotion of our Eucharistic Saviour to a little box perched on a pillar in an out-of-the-way corner of the church, or literally in an obscure hole in the wall. How correct Msgr. Gamber was in insisting that the reform that has emerged "would not have been endorsed by the majority of the Council Fathers."

The first reference to the tabernacle in a document subsequent to the Liturgy Constitution occurs in the 1964 First Instruction on the Liturgy (*Inter Oecumenici*). As this document was published less than a year after the Liturgy Constitution and while the Council was still in session, it must certainly represent the thinking of the Council Fathers. Article 95 of the document reads:

The Blessed Sacrament is to be reserved in a solid, burglar-proof tabernacle in the center of the high altar or of another altar if this is really outstanding and distinguished. Where there is a lawful custom, and in particular cases, to be approved by the local ordinary, the Blessed Sacrament may be reserved in some other place in the church; but it must be a very special place, having nobility about it, and it must be suitably decorated.

The next relevant document appears exactly a year later, on September 3, 1965, the encyclical *Mysterium Fidei* of Pope Paul VI. In this encyclical, which is a papal act and of greater authority than all the documents of Roman Congregations issued subsequently, Pope Paul VI, basing himself upon Canons 1268-1269 of the 1917 Code of Canon Law, stated: "Liturgical laws prescribe that the Blessed Sacrament be kept in churches with the greatest honor and in the most distinguished position." *Mysterium Fidei* was published while the Council was still in session. Pope Paul VI was dedicated to the teaching of the Second Vatican Council and would certainly not have taught anything which conflicted with its teaching.

It is thus beyond dispute that neither the teaching of the Liturgy Constitution nor the first two authoritative documents that deal with the sanctuary—both published while the Council was still in session—envisage the tabernacle being anywhere but in the center of the high altar or of another very distinguished altar, as the norm, except where it is already situated elsewhere by legitimate local custom.

It could be claimed with some justification that there are directives and recommendations in subsequent documents of the Holy See which authorize the moving of the tabernacle, but no requirement of Vatican II can be invoked to support them. The first of these documents is the Instruction *Eucharisticum Mysterium*, which appeared in 1967, two years after the closing of the Council. Cardinal Heenan has been quoted to the effect that the Council Fathers did not suspect that the experts who drafted the Liturgy Constitution were planning to introduce changes far more radical than those the Council Fathers had intended. Article 53 of this document provides another typical example of the technique adopted by these experts after the Council. The article is in two parts, which will be examined separately. The first reads:

> The place in a church or oratory where the Blessed Sacrament is reserved in the tabernacle should be truly prominent. It ought to be suitable for private prayer so that the faithful may easily and fruitfully, by private devotion also, continue to honor Our Lord in this Sacrament.

Two references are given for this passage. The first is to the passage from *Mysterium Fidei* which was cited above, but Pope Paul did not state that the tabernacle should be in a "truly prominent place" but in the "most prominent place" ("*in nobilissimo loco*"), which is a very different requirement. Nor did Pope Paul VI or any previous conciliar or post-conciliar document recommend that the tabernacle be

situated in a place "suitable for private prayer."
This is not simply a complete innovation but
also a misquotation of *Mysterium Fidei*. The
second source given is Article 18 of the Council's Decree on the Priestly Ministry and Life,
Presbyterorum ordinis, of December 7, 1965.
Does this document suggest that the tabernacle
should be reserved only in a "truly prominent"
rather than the "most prominent" place in the
church? Of course it does not! Does this document recommend that the tabernacle be located
in a place suitable for private prayer? Of course
it does not! This is what it *does* say:

> To carry out their pastoral duties faith-
> fully, priests need to hold daily converse
> with Christ our Lord by making visits to
> the Blessed Sacrament and by developing
> a personal devotion for the Holy
> Eucharist.

That is it. But alas, very few people ever go
to the trouble of verifying footnotes. Thus the
first sentence of Article 53 of *Eucharisticum
Mysterium* purports to show that Pope Paul VI
and the Council state that the tabernacle should
be in a place suitable for private prayer—which
they do not—and then in obedience to this
mythical requirement the next sentence reads:

> It is therefore recommended that, as far as

possible, the tabernacle be placed in a chapel distinct from the middle or central part of the church, above all in those churches where marriages and funerals take place frequently, and in places which are much visited for their artistic or historical treasures.

There is no reference for this sentence, as it is a complete innovation; and no matter how hard they may have tried, the experts could not find one source even remotely justifying this breach with tradition. It will be noted that it completely reverses the explicit teaching of the First Instruction and of the encyclical *Mysterium Fidei* that the norm should be for the tabernacle to be positioned in the center of the high altar or of another very distinguished altar and that it could be located elsewhere only as an exception. Also, note carefully that Article 53 of *Eucharisticum Mysterium* gives this as no more than a recommendation. No priest or bishop is required by it to move a single tabernacle.

But as well as being misleading, this Instruction is also self-contradictory. The very next article, No. 54, reads:

The Blessed Sacrament is to be reserved in a solid, burglar-proof tabernacle in the center of the high altar or of another altar if this is really outstanding and distinguished. Where there is a lawful custom, and in particular cases, to be approved by the local ordinary, the Blessed Sacrament may be reserved in some other place in the church; but it must be a very special place, having nobility about it, and it must be suitably decorated.

This, of course, is the rule laid down in the First Instruction.

What sort of legislation are we faced with when one paragraph recommends that as a rule the tabernacle should be placed in a chapel distinct from the center of the church and the very next stipulates that, as a rule, it must be situated on the high altar or another very distinguished altar?

Article 276 of the General Instruction on the Roman Missal, citing *Eucharisticum Mysterium* as its source, repeats the recommendation of this document that the Blessed Sacrament be reserved in a chapel suited to private adoration and prayer. But the same article states specifically that the structure of the church or legitimate local custom (*"juxta legitimas locorum consuetudines"*) can provide reasons for not doing this.

There are cathedrals, such as Westminster Cathedral in London (where the Office is sung in choir each day), where the Blessed Sacrament has always been reserved in a separate chapel. But in a cathedral or church where the tabernacle has always been placed upon the high altar—a practice praised and commended by Pope Pius XII and Pope Paul VI—to move it from this central place of honor can only be seen as a demotion of the Blessed Sacrament.

THE NEW CODE OF CANON LAW (1983) AND THE CATECHISM OF THE CATHOLIC CHURCH (1994)

The New Code of Canon Law (1983) contains no legislation requiring the tabernacle to be demoted from the center of the high altar, even though it does not state specifically that it should be placed there. Canon 938-§2 states:

> The tabernacle in which the Most Holy Eucharist is reserved should be placed in a part of the church that is prominent, conspicuous, beautifully decorated and suitable for prayer.

There is no place in a church that is more prominent and suitable for prayer than the high altar (if it has not been destroyed).

The latest pronouncement concerning the tabernacle can be found in the *Catechism of the Catholic Church* (1994). It states that "the tabernacle should be located in an especially worthy place in the church, and should be constructed in such a way that it emphasizes and manifests the truth of the real presence of Christ in the Blessed Sacrament." (No. 1379). In No. 1183 the Catechism quotes the encyclical *Mysterium Fidei* of Pope Paul VI: "The tabernacle is to be situated 'in churches in a most worthy place with the greatest honor.'" The Latin original "*in nobilissimo loco*" is better translated as "*the* most worthy place"—which, as *Mysterium Fidei* states explicitly, is the center of the high altar. The official English text of the encyclical published by the Catholic Truth Society of England and Wales in 1965 translates "*in nobilissimo loco*" as "the most distinguished position." In view of the fact that the Catechism cites *Mysterium Fidei*, it is not unreasonable to claim that it recommends the center of the high altar as the most appropriate place for the tabernacle. No. 1183 also states, referring to No. 128 of the Liturgy Constitution of Vatican Council II: "The dignity, placing and security of the Eucharistic tabernacle should foster adoration before the Lord really present in the Blessed Sacrament of the altar." The dignity of the tabernacle is best affirmed by placing it in the center of the high altar.

RETURN TO
THE ALTAR OF SACRIFICE

How tragic it is that the objectives of what Pope Pius XII condemned as a "wicked movement" are now being imposed upon us as the norm for Catholic worship. See that your flocks are not deceived, he warned, "by a mania for restoring primitive usages in the liturgy."

It was under the guise of a return to the primitive that the Protestant Reformers were able to destroy the Mass. Today, in the service of false ecumenism, the Catholic ethos of our churches is being replaced by a Protestant ethos, precisely under the guise of a return to earlier practices. No good fruits have come from this ecumenical surrender. In no country in the western world have the changes been followed by an increase in fervor and piety among the faithful—only by a massive falling away from the Faith.[21]

Msgr. Klaus Gamber certainly agrees with Cardinal Ratzinger (page 27 above) that the change to Mass facing the people was a mistake. He has even stated that a return to traditional belief in the Eucharist will only come about with a return to the traditional altar:

A real change in the contemporary perception of the purpose of the Mass and the

Eucharist will occur only when the table altars are removed and Mass is again celebrated at the high altar; when the purpose of the Mass is again seen as an act of adoration and glorification of God and of offering thanks for His blessings, for our salvation and for the promise of the heavenly life to come, and as the mystical reenactment of the Lord's sacrifice on the cross.[22]

St. Richard Gwyn, a Welsh teacher and father of six children who was executed in 1584 for recusancy (refusal to attend Protestant services), looked upon the desecrated sanctuaries of Wales and remarked with sadness: *"Yn lle allor, trestyl trist"*—"In place of an altar, there is a miserable table." God grant that the "miserable tables" that have replaced the traditional altars of sacrifice throughout the Catholic world will one day themselves be removed and replaced by traditional altars of sacrifice. God grant too that the traditional liturgy of the Mass will be restored together with the traditional altars, so that our priests can once again begin the Holy Sacrifice of the Mass with the timeless words, *"Introibo ad altare Dei,"* and so that a manifestly sacrificial rite of Mass will be offered once more upon a manifestly sacrificial altar.

NOTES

1. Martin Luther, *Against Henry, King of England,* 1522, *Werke,* Vol. X, p. 220.

2. J. Hooper, *Later Writings* (Cambridge: Parker Society, 1852), p. 32.

3. E. Duffy, *The Stripping of the Altars* (New Haven, CT: Yale University Press, 1992), p. 480.

4. J. Calvin, *Institutes of the Christian Religion,* Book IV, xviii, n. 12 (London, 1838), Vol. II, p. 526.

5. P. Hughes, *The Reformation in England,* Vol. II (London, 1950), p. 121.

6. Thomas Cranmer, *Works*, Vol. II (Cambridge: Parker Society, 1846), pp. 524-525.

7. J. G. Ridley, *Nicholas Ridley* (London, 1957), pp. 218-219.

8. T. E. Bridgett, C.S.S.R., *A History of the Eucharist in Great Britain* (London: Burns & Oates, 1908), p. 63.

9. Duffy, *op. cit.,* p. 465.

10. Hughes, *op. cit.,* p. 111.

11. Cited in Testimonial by Msgr. W. Nyssen in Klaus Gamber, *The Reform of the Roman Liturgy* (Roman Catholic Books, P.O. Box 255, Harrison, NY 10528, 1993), p. xiii.

12. Gamber, *The Reform of the Roman Liturgy ,* p. 61.

13. J. Heenan, *A Crown of Thorns* (London: Hodder & Stoughton, 1974), p. 367.

14. *Catholic Standard* (Dublin), October 17, 1973.

15. Ralph Wiltgen, *The Rhine Flows into the Tiber* (1967; rpt. Rockford, Illinois: TAN, 1985), p. 210.

16. Michael Davies, *Pope Paul's New Mass* (Angelus Press, 2918 Tracy Ave., Kansas City, Missouri 64109, 1980), Appendix III.

17. *Notitiae* (journal of the *Consilium*), Rome, September-October, 1965.

18. Gamber, *op. cit.,* p. 142.

19. *30 Days,* June 1993, pp. 67-68.

20. *Eucharisticum Mysterium,* Instruction of the Sacred Congregation of Rites on the Eucharistic Mystery, May 25, 1967, par. 55.

21. Cf. Michael Davies, *Liturgical Shipwreck: 20 Years of the New Mass* (TAN, 1995), pp. 27-29.

22. Gamber, *op. cit.,* p. 175.